The Open University

AA100
The Arts Past and Present

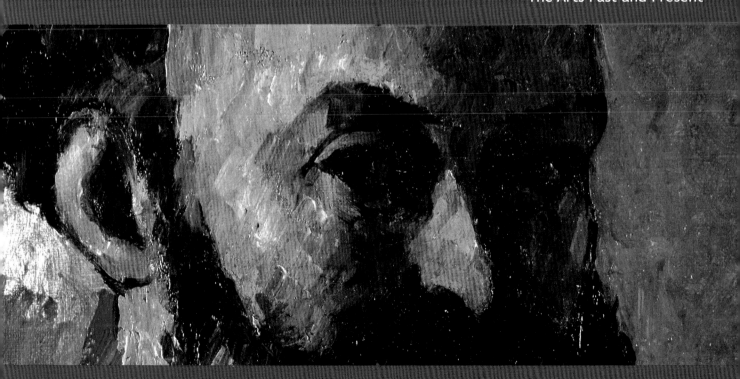

Illustration Book

Plates for Books 1 and 2

This publication forms part of an Open University course AA100 The Arts Past and Present. Details of this and other Open University courses can be obtained from the Student Registration and Enquiry Service, The Open University, PO Box 197, Milton Keynes MK7 6BJ, United Kingdom: tel. +44 (0)845 300 60 90, email general-enquiries@open.ac.uk

Alternatively, you may visit the Open University website at http://www.open.ac.uk where you can learn more about the wide range of courses and packs offered at all levels by The Open University.

To purchase a selection of Open University course materials visit http://www.ouw.co.uk, or contact Open University Worldwide, Walton Hall, Milton Keynes MK7 6AA, United Kingdom for a brochure. tel. +44 (0)1908 858793; fax +44 (0)1908 858787; email ouw-customer-services@open.ac.uk

Cover image: Paul Cézanne, self-portrait, 1879, oil on canvas. Oskar Reinhart Collection, Winterthur. Photo: akg-images.

The Open University
Walton Hall, Milton Keynes
MK7 6AA

First published 2008

Edited and designed by The Open University.

Typeset by The Open University.

Printed and bound in the United Kingdom by Spin Offset Ltd., Rainham, Essex.

ISBN 9780749217044

1.1

Contents

Book 2   *Tradition and Dissent*

Plate 1.3.1 Paul Cézanne, *Still Life, Curtain, Jug and Compotier*. c.1893–94, oil on canvas, 59 x 72 cm. Private collection, USA. Photo: akg-images/Erich Lessing.

Plate 1.3.2 Camille Pissarro, *Hoarfrost, the Old Road to Ennery*, 1873, oil on canvas, 65 x 93 cm. Musée d'Orsay, Paris.
Photo: © RMN/Hervé Lewandowski.

Plate 1.3.3 Paul Cézanne, *The House of the Hanged Man at Auvers*, 1872–73, oil on canvas, 55 x 66 cm, Musée d'Orsay, Paris. Photo: © RMN/Hervé Lewandowski.

Plate 1.3.4　Paul Cézanne, *Bathers*, 1874–75, oil on canvas, 38 x 46 cm. Metropolitan Museum of Art, New York. The Metropolitan Museum of Art, Bequest of Joan Whitney Payson, 1975 (1976.201.12). Photograph by Malcolm Varon. Photo: © 1984 The Metropolitan Museum of Art.

Plate 1.3.5 Paul Cézanne, *Bathers*, c. 1894–1906, oil on canvas, 133 x 195 cm. The National Gallery, London. Purchased with a special grant and the aid of the Max Rayne Foundation, 1964. Photo: © The National Gallery, London.

Plate 1.3.6 Palma Vecchio, *Bathing Nymphs*, c.1525/8, oil on canvas, 78 x 124 cm. Kunsthistorisches Museum, Vienna.

Plate 1.3.7 Jean-Honoré Fragonard, *Baigneuses*, c.1765, oil on canvas, 64 x 80 cm. Musée du Louvre, Paris. Photo: © RMN/ © All rights reserved.

Plate 1.3.8 Correggio, *Leda with the Swan*, c.1532, oil on canvas, 152 x 191 cm. Gemäldegalerie, Berlin. © 2007 bpk/ Gemäldegalerie, Staatliche Museen zu Berlin. Photo: Jörg P. Anders.

Plate 1.3.9 Paul Cézanne, *Leda and the Swan*, *c*.1886–90, oil on canvas, 60 x 73 cm. BF36, Barnes Foundation, Merion, Philadelphia. Photo: © reproduced with the permission of The Barnes Foundation™. All rights reserved.

Plate 1.3.10 Pablo Picasso, *Bathers in a Forest*, 1907, gouache, watercolour and pencil 48 × 58 cm. Philadelphia Museum of Art: The Samuel S. White III and Vera White Collection, 1967. Photo: © Succession Picasso/DACS, London 2007.

Plate 1.3.11 Henri Matisse, *Bathers with a Turtle*, 1908, oil on canvas, 182 x 221 cm. © Succession H Matisse/DACS, London 2007. Photo: © Saint Louis Art Museum, Missouri/The Bridgeman Art Library.

Plate 1.3.12 William-Adolphe Bouguereau, *Bathers*, 1884, oil on canvas, 201 x 129 cm. A. A. Munger Collection, 1901.458, The Art Institute of Chicago. Photo: © The Art Institute of Chicago.

Plate 1.3.13   Paul Cézanne, *The Three Bathers*, *c*.1879–82, oil on canvas, 52 x 55 cm. Musée de la Ville de Paris, Musée du Petit-Palais, Giraudon/The Bridgeman Art Library.

Plate 1.3.14   Paul Cézanne, *Academic Study of a Nude Male Model*, *c*.1865, black chalk on
paper with white highlight, 31 x 49 cm. Fitzwilliam Museum, Cambridge. Photo: © Fitzwilliam Museum,
Cambridge.

Plate 1.3.15   Paul Cézanne, *Madame Cézanne (Hortense Fiquet) with Hortensias*, c.1885, graphite and watercolour on paper, 31 x 46 cm. Private collection.

Plate 1.3.16 Edouard Manet, *Olympia*, 1863, oil on canvas, 130 x 190 cm. Musée d'Orsay, Paris. Photo: © RMN/Jean-Gilles Berizzi.

Plate 1.3.17 Paul Cézanne, *A Modern Olympia*, 1873, oil on canvas, 46 x 55 cm. Musée d'Orsay, Paris. Photo: © RMN/ Hervé Lewandowski.

Plate 1.3.18   Constantin Guys, *Trois Femmes près d'un comptoir*, 1860, pen and wash with watercolour, 25 x 18 cm. Musée du Petit Palais, Paris. Photo: © Photothèque des Musée de la Ville de Paris/Pierrain.

Plate 1.3.19 Paul Cézanne, *Three Bathers*, 1875–77, oil on canvas, 31 x 33 cm. Private collection. Formerly collection of Henry Moore.

Plate 1.3.20 Paul Cézanne, *Mont Sainte-Victoire with Large Pine*, c.1887, oil on canvas. 67 x 92 cm. The Samuel Courtauld Trust, Courtauld Institute of Art Gallery, London/The Bridgeman Art Library.

Plate 1.3.21 Nicholas Poussin, *Landscape with a Calm*, 1650–51, oil on canvas, 126 x 161 cm. The J. Paul Getty Museum, Los Angeles.

Plate 1.3.22 Paul Cézanne, *Mont Sainte-Victoire from Les Lauves*, 1904–06, oil on canvas, 60 x 72 cm. Kunstmuseum, Basel. Inv. Nr. G 1955.12. Photo: Kunstmuseum Basel, Martin Bühler.

Plate 1.3.23   Paul Cézanne, *Diver in Moonlight*, 1867–70, pencil, watercolour and gouache on paper, 16 x 16 cm. National Museum of Wales, Amgueddfa Genedlaethol Cymru.

Plate 1.3.24 Paul Cézanne, *Jug and Fruit*, 1885–87, oil on canvas, 43 × 63 cm. Private Collection. Photo: © Lefevre Fine Art Ltd., London/The Bridgeman Art Library.

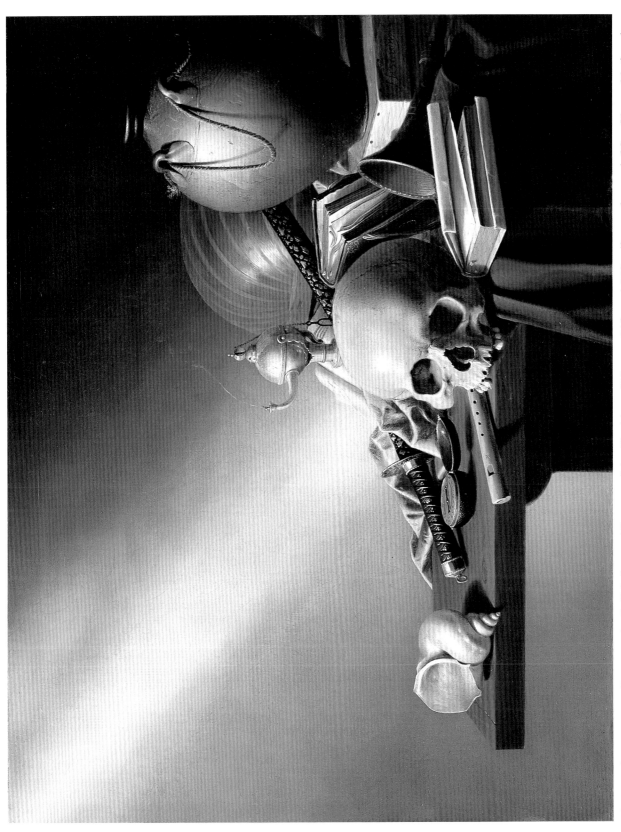

Plate 1.3.25 Harmen Steenwyck, *Still Life: an Allegory of the Vanities of Human Life*, c. 1650, oil on oak panel, 39 x 51 cm. National Gallery, London. Presented by Lord Savile, 1888. Photo: © The National Gallery, London.

Plate 1.3.26 Jacob van Hulsdonck, *Still Life*, 1620–40, oil on panel, 42 x 50 cm. The J. Paul Getty Museum, Los Angeles.

Plate 1.3.27 Louise Moillon, *Still Life with Bowl of Curaçao Oranges*, 1634, oil on panel, 46 x 65 cm. F.1972.38.P. The Norton Simon Foundation, Pasadena.

Plate 1.3.28   Jean-Siméon Chardin, *The Buffet*, 1728, oil on canvas, 194 x 129 cm. Musée du Louvre, Paris. Photo: © RMN/Jean-Gilles Berizzi.

Plate 1.3.29 Jean-Siméon Chardin, *The Fast-Day Meal*, 1731, oil on copper, 33 x 41 cm. Musée du Louvre, Paris. Photo: © RMN/Gérard Blot/Hervé Lewandowski.

Plate 1.3.30 Francisco de Zurbarán, *Still Life with Lemons, Oranges and a Rose*, 1633, oil on canvas, 84 x 131 cm (framed). F.1972.06.P. The Norton Simon Foundation, Pasadena.

34

Plate 1.3.31 Henri Matisse, *Still Life with Green Sideboard*, 1928, oil on canvas, 82 × 100 cm. Musée National d'Art Moderne, Centre Georges Pompidou, Paris. Photo: © CNAC/MNAM Dist. RMN/© Jacqueline Hyde. © Succession H Matisse/DACS, London 2007.

Plate 1.3.32   Paul Cézanne, *Still Life with Plaster Cast*, *c*.1894, oil on paper and mounted on panel, 71 x 57 cm. The Samuel Courtauld Trust, Courtauld Institute of Art Gallery, London.

Plate 1.3.33 Paul Cézanne, *Still Life with Pot of Flowers and Pears*, 1880–90, oil on canvas, 46 x 56 cm. The Samuel Courtauld Trust, Courtauld Institute of Art Gallery, London.

Plate 1.3.34 Paul Cézanne, *Still Life with Apples*, 1893–94, oil on canvas, 66 x 82 cm. The J. Paul Getty Museum, Los Angeles.

Plate 1.3.35 Paul Cézanne, *Landscape with Mont Sainte-Victoire*, c.1890, oil on canvas, 65 x 92 cm. Musée d'Orsay, Paris. Photo: © RMN / © Hervé Lewandowski.

Plate 1.3.36   Paul Cézanne, *The Grounds of the Chateau Noir*, *c.*1900-04, oil on canvas, 91 x 71 cm.
Tate Gallery, London (on loan from the National Gallery, London). Photo: © National Gallery, London.

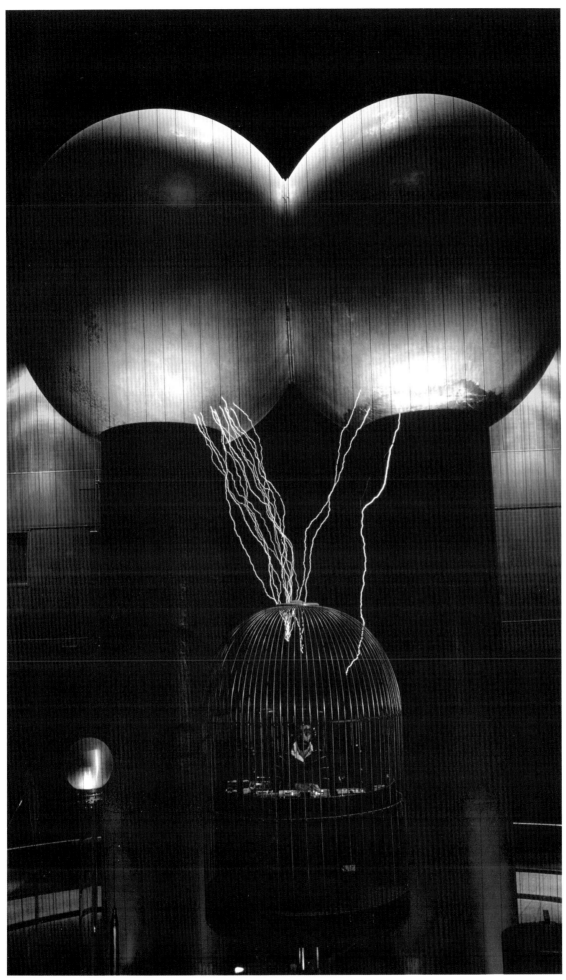

Plate 1.4.1 Faraday Cage with Van de Graaf generator. Boston Museum of Science, USA.
Photo: Peter Menzel/Science Photo Library.

Plate 1.5.1 Unknown artist, 'The Socialist competition transforms work into a matter of honour, glory and heroism', 1931, poster. Photo: Photo12.com – JSR/DR.

KEKSA CALLAR, JAŞ GODAKLAR BAXTIJAR,
BAXTIJARLAR VATANIDIR BU DIJAR.
(„KPK qurocilarnin ortaq STALINGA tasrigi" dan)

МЫ—РОДИНА САМЫХ СЧАСТЛИВЫХ, ОТВАЖНЫХ,
ВСЕСИЛЬНЫХ ЛЮДЕЙ,
ГДЕ ВЕСЕЛЫ СТАРЦЫ СЕДЫЕ, ГДЕ СМЕХ БЕЗЗАБОТЕН ДЕТЕЙ.
(Из приветствия строителей БФК тов. СТАЛИНУ)

Plate 1.5.2   Unknown artist, 'Moscow by Stalin' (1), poster. Photo: © Thomas Johnson/Sygma/CORBIS.

Plate 1.5.3 Unknown artist, 'Moscow by Stalin' (2), poster. Photo: © Thomas Johnson/Sygma/CORBIS.

Plate 1.5.4 V. I. Govorkov, 'We will vanquish drought', 1950, poster. Photo: SCR Photo Library.

Plate 1.5.5 Metal folder with Stalin's portraits, 1949. State Historical Museum, Moscow. Inventory #: CN-56.

Plate 1.5.6   Unknown artist, 'Proletarians of all the Country, Unite!', carpet. State Historical Museum, Moscow. Inventory #: RP-1527.

Plate 1.5.7 Ink set for Stalin's seventieth anniversary from the military division 01773 with inscription 'To the Chief and Teacher of the Soviet People', 1949, made from ammunition. The State Central Museum of Contemporary History of Russia, Moscow. Inventory #: 16 1554.

Plate 1.5.8   Unknown artist, 'From the wives and workers of Kiev experimental plant', 1939, carpet. The State Central Museum of Contemporary History of Russia, Moscow. Inventory #: 16336/9.

Plate 2.2.1   William Blake, title page from *Songs of Innocence and Of Experience*, *c*.1802–08, relief etching finished in ink and watercolour, 11 x 7 cm. Fitzwilliam Museum, Cambridge.
Photo: Bridgeman Art Library.

Plate 2.2.2   William Blake, 'The Fly', plate 41 from *Songs of Innocence and Of Experience*, *c*.1802–08, relief etching finished in ink and watercolour, 11 x 7 cm. Fitzwilliam Museum, Cambridge.
Photo: Bridgeman Art Library.

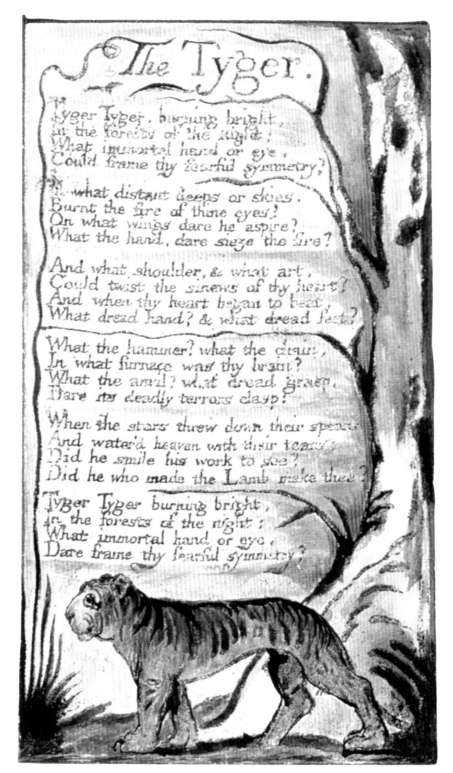

Plate 2.2.3   William Blake, 'The Tyger', plate 43 from *Songs of Innocence and Of Experience*, *c*.1802–08, relief etching finished in ink and watercolour, 11 x 7 cm. Fitzwilliam Museum, Cambridge. Photo: Bridgeman Art Library.

Plate 2.2.4   William Blake, 'The Lamb', plate 7 from *Songs of Innocence and Of Experience*, *c*.1789–94, relief etching finished in pen and watercolour, 11 x 7 cm. Fitzwilliam Museum, Cambridge. Photo: Bridgeman Art Library.

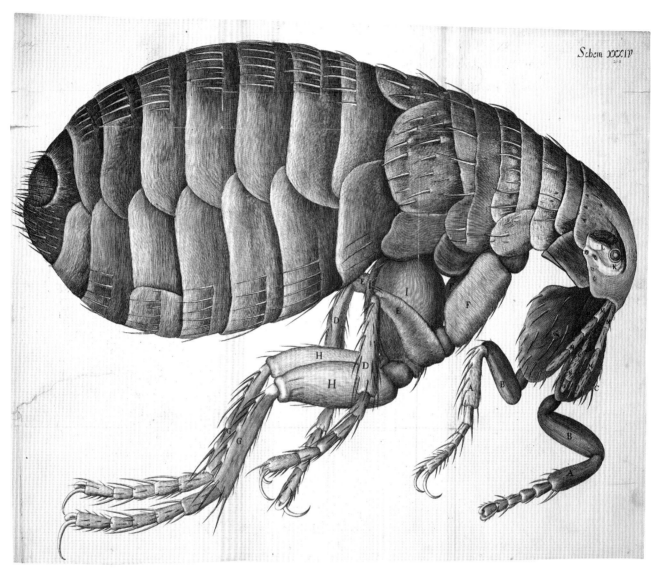

Plate 2.2.6   Workshop of the Boucicaut Master, miniature painting showing the battle of Crécy between the English and the French (26 August 1346) from the illuminated manuscript *Grandes Chroniques de France*, *c*.1415. British Library, London, Cotton Nero E. II pt.2 f.152v. Photo: The British Library.

coytat enim amozem psttne delectationis indolozem contrition
nis. Ecce qualit p naturam uolucrum doceri potest inta religi
osozum.

De miluo.

Miluus mollis t uiribz t uo
latu · quasi mollis auis.
unde t nuncupat rapacissimum.
ch t semp domesticis auibz insidi
atur. Sicut enim in libro ethimo
logiarum ysidor legit · miluus
a molli uolatu nominat. Est enim
miluus moll uiribz. Illos au mil
uus significat quos mollices uoluptates temptant. C ad auentz
miluus uestit: ct carnalibz desidijs uoluptuosi delectant. Cirta
coquinas t macella miluus assidue uolitat. ut siquid crude
carnis ab eis piciat fozis · ueloci rapiat. P hoc enim miluus eos
nob innuit. quos cura uentris sollicitos reddit. Q g huius mundi
sunt. uoluptuosa querunt. macella frequentant t coquinis in
hiant. cq miluus timidus e in magnis: audax in minimis. Sil
uestres uolucres rape non audet. domesticas aute insidiari so
let. Insidiat pullis ut illos rapiat. t quos incautos reppit · uelo
cius necat. Sic molles t uoluptuosi teneros pullos rapiunt: qa
simpliciores t indiscretos suis moribz aptant. t ad pravos usus p
trahunt. Sup eos lente uolando incautos decipiunt. dum eos
blandis sermonibz adulando seducunt. Ecce quoru uolucres q
ratione carent pravos homines t ratione intentos p exempla per
uerse opationis docent.

De psitaco

Sola india mittit auem psitacum colore uiridi torque pu
nicea. grandi lingua. t ceteris auibz latiore. unde t articu
lata uerba exprimit. ita ut si eam non uidis. hominem loq putes.

Plate 2.2.7 Unknown artist, miniature painting of a kite from the illuminated manuscript *The Aberdeen Bestiary*, c.1200. Aberdeen University Library. Photo: University of Aberdeen.

Plate 2.2.8 David Herbert Lawrence, *The Lizard*, 1928, watercolour, 30 x 22 cm. Lost original. Photo: © Keith Sagar.

Plate 2.4.1 Joseph Mallord William Turner, *The Burning of the Houses of Lords and Commons, October 16, 1834*, 1834 or 1835, oil on canvas, 92 x 123 cm. Philadelphia Museum of Art, M1928-1-41. Photo: Philadelphia Museum of Art: The John Howard McFadden Collection, 1928.

Plate 2.4.2   Hardwick Hall, Derbyshire, built in sixteenth century.   Photo: © NTPL/Mike Williams.

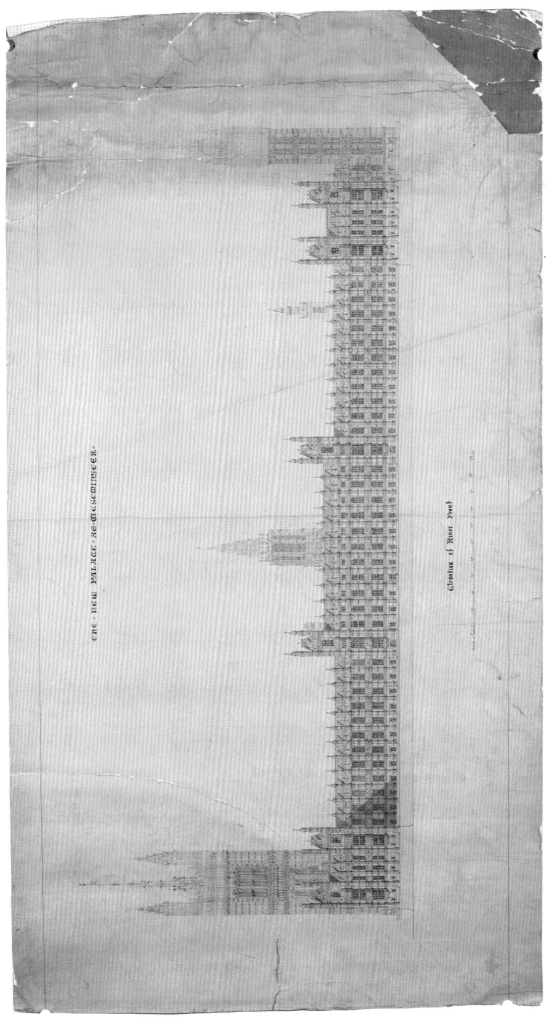

Plate 2.4.3 Charles Barry, *Elevation of the River Front*, adopted competition design for the new Houses of Parliament, 1836, drawing. RIBA Library, London, 12337. Photo: RIBA Library Drawings and Archives Collections.

Plate 2.4.4 John Chessel Buckler, *Perspective of the River Front*, competition design for the new Houses of Parliament, which was awarded second prize, 1835. The National Archives, Kew, WORK29/47. Photo: The National Archives UK.

FONTHILL ABBEY.

VIEW OF THE WEST, & NORTH FRONTS.

From the End of the Clerks Walk

Plate 2.4.5   T. Higham after J. Martin, 'Fonthill Abbey, View of the West and North Fronts from the End of the Clerk's Walk', lithograph from Rutter, J. (1823) *Delineations of Fonthill and its Abbey*, London, plate xi, p. 66. The British Library, London. 191.e.6. Photo: © The British Library Board. All Rights Reserved.

Plate 2.4.6 Chamber of the House of Lords, Palace of Westminster, looking towards the throne, completed 1847. Photo: Derry Moore Photography.

CHAPEL ROYAL BRIGHTON

Sᵀ GEORGE'S CHAPEL WINSOR

CONTRASTED ROYAL CHAPELS

Plate 2.4.7 A.W.N. Pugin, 'Contrasted Royal Chapels', etching from Pugin, A.W.N. (1836) *Contrasts, or, a parallel between the noble edifices of the fourteenth and fifteenth centuries and similar buildings of the present day; shewing the present decay of taste*, London. British Library, London, 560*.d.32. Photo: © The British Library Board. All Rights Reserved.

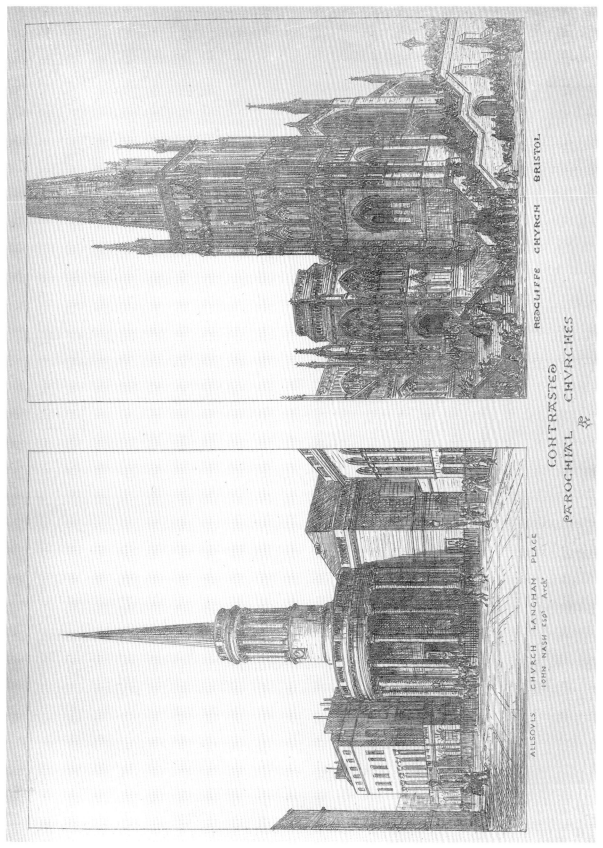

CONTRASTED
PAROCHIAL CHVRCHES

ALLSOVLS CHVRCH LANGHAM PLACE
JOHN NASH ESQ.ʳ Archᵗ

REDCLIFFE CHVRCH BRISTOL

Plate 2.4.8 A.W.N. Pugin, 'Contrasted Parochial Churches', etching from Pugin, A.W.N. (1836) *Contrasts, or; a parallel between the noble edifices of the fourteenth and fifteenth centuries and similar buildings of the present day; shewing the present decay of taste*, London. British Library, London, 560*.d.32. Photo: © The British Library Board. All Rights Reserved.

Plate 2.4.9   A.W.N. Pugin, 'Contrasted Chapels', etching from Pugin, A.W.N. (1836) *Contrasts, or, a parallel between the noble edifices of the fourteenth and fifteenth centuries and similar buildings of the present day; shewing the present decay of taste*, London. British Library, London, 560*.d.32. Photo: © The British Library Board. All Rights Reserved. Despite being labelled as 'St Pancras Chapel' this is, in fact, St Mary, Somers Town, 1822-26 by W. and H.W. Inwood.

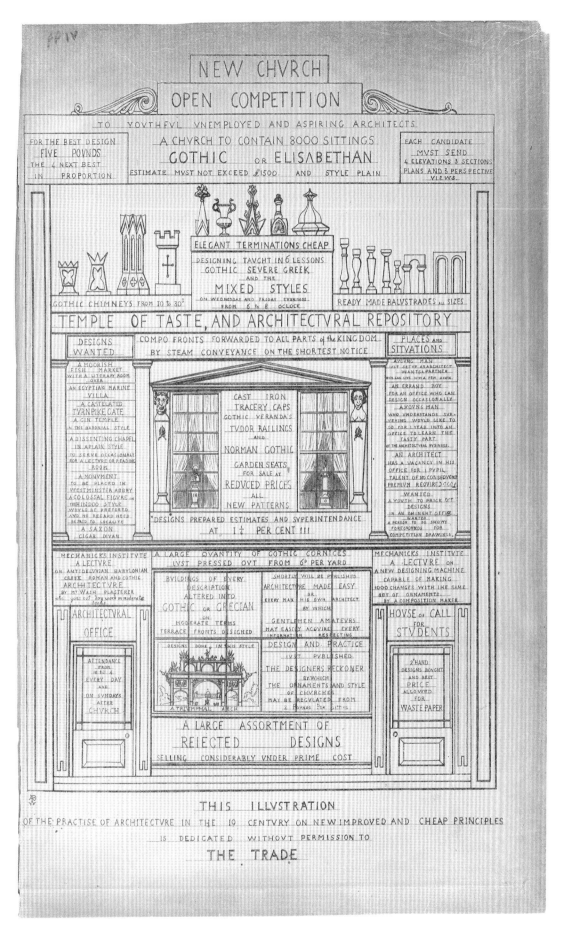

Plate 2.4.10   A.W.N. Pugin, 'This Illustration of the Practise of Architecture in the
19 Century on New Improved and Cheap Principles is dedicated without Permission to
The Trade', etching from Pugin, A.W.N. (1836) *Contrasts, or, a parallel between the noble
edifices of the fourteenth and fifteenth centuries and similar buildings of the present day;
shewing the present decay of taste*, London. British Library, London, 560*.d.32.
Photo: © The British Library Board. All Rights Reserved.

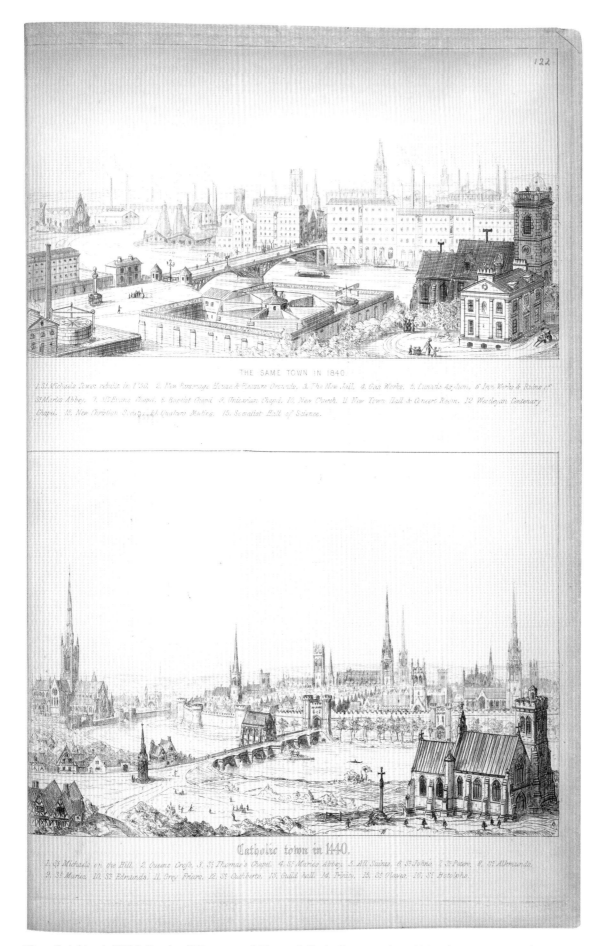

THE SAME TOWN IN 1840

1. St Michaels Tower rebuilt in 1750. 2. New Parsonage House & Pleasure Grounds. 3. The New Jail. 4. Gas Works. 5. Lunatic Asylum. 6. Iron Works & Ruins of St Maries Abbey. 7. St Evans Chapel. 8. Baptist Chapel. 9. Unitarian Chapel. 10. New Church. 11 New Town Hall & Concert Room. 12 Wesleyan Centenary Chapel. 13. New Christian Society. 14 Quakers Meeting. 15. Socialist Hall of Science.

Catholic town in 1440.

1. St Michaels on the Hill. 2. Queens Cross. 3. St Thomas's Chapel. 4. St Maries Abbey. 5. All Saints. 6. St Johns. 7. St Peters. 8. St Alkmunds. 9. St Maries. 10. St Edmunds. 11. Grey Friars. 12. St Cuthberts. 13. Guild hall. 14. Trinity. 15. St Olaves. 16. St Botolphs.

Plate 2.4.11   A.W.N. Pugin, '[Contrasted Towns] Catholic town in 1440. The same town in 1840', lithograph from Pugin, A.W.N. (1841) *Contrasts, or, a parallel between the noble edifices of the fourteenth and fifteenth centuries and similar buildings of the present day; shewing the present decay of taste*, London. British Library, London, 560*.d.33. Photo: © The British Library Board. All Rights Reserved.

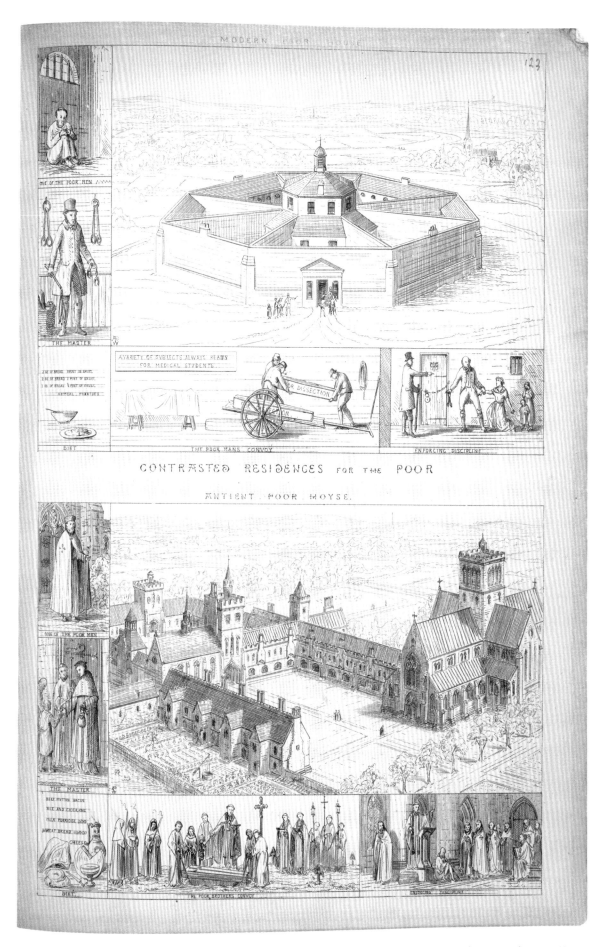

CONTRASTED RESIDENCES FOR THE POOR

Plate 2.4.12   A.W.N. Pugin, 'Contrasted Residences for the Poor', lithograph from Pugin, A.W.N. (1841) *Contrasts, or, a parallel between the noble edifices of the fourteenth and fifteenth centuries and similar buildings of the present day; shewing the present decay of taste*, London. British Library, London, 560*.d.33. Photo: © The British Library Board. All Rights Reserved.

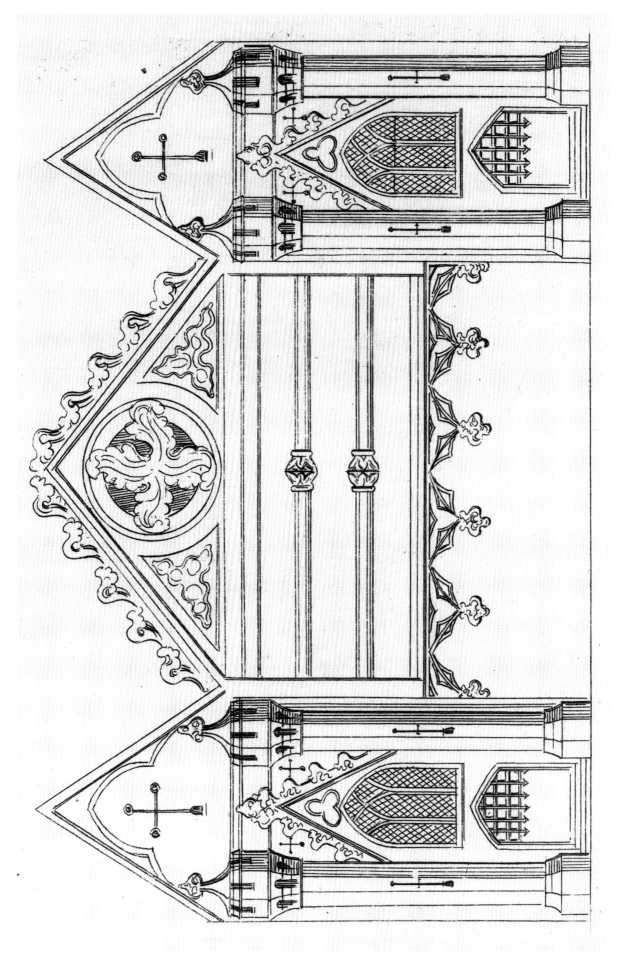

Plate 2.4.13 A.W.N. Pugin, 'New Sheffield pattern for a modern Castellated Grate', engraving from Pugin, A.W.N (1841) *The True Principles of Pointed or Christian Architecture*, London, John Weale, p. 23. British Library, London, 786.k.29. Photo: © The British Library Board. All Rights Reserved.

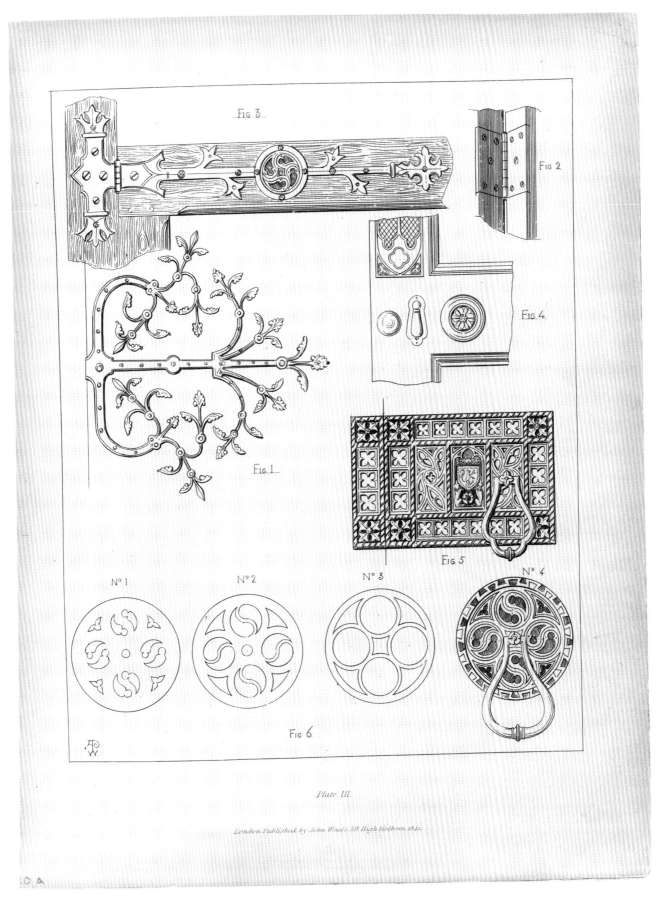

Plate 2.4.14   A.W.N. Pugin, 'Plate III', engraving from Pugin, A.W.N. (1841) *The True Principles of Pointed or Christian Architecture*, London: John Weale. British Library, London, 786.k.29. Photo: © The British Library Board. All Rights Reserved.

Plate 2.4.15   Bernt Notke, rood screen, 1470-77, oak. Lübeck Cathedral. Photo: Helge Schenk, Hamburg.

Plate 2.4.16   Bernt Notke, detail of Mary Magdalen, rood screen, 1470-77, oak. Lübeck Cathedral.
Photo: Helge Schenk, Hamburg.

Plate 2.4.17   Unknown artist, Christ on the Cross from former rood screen, *c*.1510–20, polychromed wood, life size. Saint Chads Roman Catholic Cathedral, Birmingham. Photo: Malcolm Daisley, e-motif photography.

Plate 2.4.18 Antwerp carved wooden altarpiece (open), 1518–22. Marienkirche, Lübeck.
Photo: Helge Schenk, Hamburg.

Plate 2.4.19 Antwerp carved wooden altarpiece (half open), painted shutters by the so-called Master of 1518,
1518–22. Marienkirche, Lübeck. Photo: Helge Schenk, Hamburg.

Plate 2.4.20 Antwerp carved wooden altarpiece (closed),1518–22, 286 x 254 cm. Marienkirche, Lübeck. Photo: Helge Schenk, Hamburg.

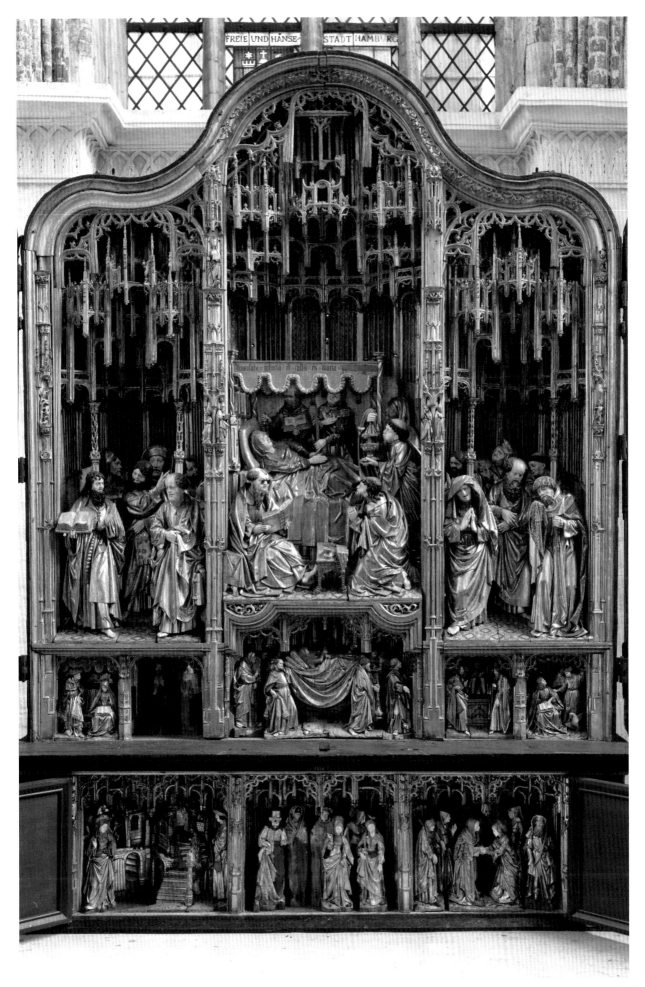

Plate 2.4.21   Antwerp carved wooden altarpiece (central panel and predella), 1518–22. Marienkirche, Lübeck.
Photo: Helge Schenk, Hamburg.

Plate 2.4.22   Unknown artist, carved wooden altarpiece, *c*.1510-20, oak, 200 x 214 cm. Saint Giles Roman Catholic church, Cheadle, Staffordshire. Photo: Malcolm Daisley, e-motif photography.

Plate 2.4.23   Unknown artist, cupboard door with angel, *c.*1480, oak, 35 x 28 cm. Oscott College, Birmingham.
Photo: Malcolm Daisley, e-motif photography.

Plate 2.4.24 Unknown artist, altar, the Side Chapel, Hospital of Saint John, Alton, Staffordshire. Photo: Malcolm Daisley, e-motif photography.